From the City of Shem

by

Nadja

NadjaMedia.com

NadjaMedia.com

Nadja Media

530 Los Angeles Ave., Suite 115
Moorpark, California 93021

ISBN-10: 1942057008

ISBN-13: 978-1-942057-00-0

This is a work of fiction. Names, characters, places, and incidents either are a product of the author's imagination or are used fictitiously, and any resemblance to actual persons, living or dead, business establishments, events, or locales is entirely coincidental. No liability is assumed for damages resulting from the use of or misinterpretation of information contained herein. The information is meant as a guideline only and to help Humanity better reflect upon themselves, where they have been, where they are now, and where they potentially may be going.

Dedication

To all those kindred souls who are in love with

life, Mother Earth, and honor the

Source of All Creation.

— Nadja

Acknowledgments

With gratitude to all the poets from all over the

world and to as far back as history reaches.

They connect us to our Souls and our Hearts.

Introduction

This is Nadja's first collection of poetry which spans several decades. It is reminiscent of classical poets of transcendental quality. The 72 selections are spiritually, metaphysically based and many create joy in the hearts of the readers. Nadja draws upon nature and the soul for her inspiration which is evident in her writing.

Contents

From the

City of Shem

by

Nadja

Reflection

What inspires me to sing

Also makes the raven call

The lily to breathe forth joy

And the eye of the doe

Soft and tender

Everywhere I look I see

The spark in me reflected back again

The wren's song

The ocean breeze

The daffodil

The sky

All sing in harmony with me

Reflection

The redwood tree

The mighty oak

Stand tall and with their

Driving force

Reach up through space

To make their Presence known

They too know

From whence they came

And you, My Love, echo back to me

God's very song

And through your eye

I enter heaven

Pot of Gold

Have you ever listened to the rainbow

Play its music upon the sky

And heard the symphony of colors

Weave upon themselves

The Song of Joy?

Bird Song

A bird Is

And in this state

It sings

Music

As the artist plucks

The strings of his guitar

He awakens their reflection

Within my Being

Limbless parts of me

Begin to dance

And a new composition

Has made its debut

Servants All

We all serve

Do not be blinded

By personality, status, intellect, circumstance

For even the most vile of men,

Unknowingly,

Serves to polish the Soul of others

So like the bacteria of disease

Which perform their Duty

In returning flesh to Earth

Also serve they who only stand and wait

But the goal is to serve

With conscious awareness

Servants All

For it is in this state

That we can give treasures

Of everlasting worth

Temporarily Out of Service

The whirlwinds of life

Suck me under

And give me a good thrashing

Until I awake again

To the knowing

That Love IS

Observer

If we could but be still

And watch the pageant of Life

From detached view

We would see how beautifully interwoven

Are the events and people

In each ones sphere of life

It is a tapestry, a dance

Which at times appears to be of angels' breath

And at others, of the devil's fiery tongue

But nonetheless

It is a dance

Done on the shores of karma

Observer

Upon the Sea of Life

Each one is here to dance his own dance

Which only he alone can do

Stand back and watch

And you will be filled

With wonder

And with quiet joy

Invitation

Use me freely

As Thy Instrument

And I will play

Thy Song

Upon my harp

Forever

Development

Unfoldment

Life grows

Spirit IS

We are

I AM

Disciple

The Fisherman cast His line into the River

Many fish were attracted to His bait

Finally one bit

And discovered it was securely hooked

The fish swam off course

And played in endless circles

The Fisherman allowed His line to go slack

And gave the fish the freedom to do as it pleased

However, free as the fish felt

It knew that the Fisherman knew

And that He was patiently waiting

If needs be for Eternity

Disciple

For the fish to play out what it must

At last the fish gave up in exhaustion

It submitted

And the Fisherman reeled it slowly in

Toward

Its

Destiny

Ancient One

Eyes like diamonds

Skin like wood

Old age revealed

Life understood

Reaction

The cherry tree

Exploded into blossom

While riding this current

I, too, burst open

Like an eager flower

Celebration

For my wedding

I will clothe my body

In a cloak of white light

And lay aside

The garments

Of this world

Bedtime

My eyes are heavy with sleep

My limbs are tired and ache

My mind cannot go deep

But my Spirit is ever awake

H. Wren

The House Wren

Is one of my favorite birds

Its song is powerful

And gushes forth upon the ear

Like a colossal

Waterfall of Joy

Whoever thought

That glory such as this

With force to break

Into a thousand heavens

Could abide within

This tiny mite of bird?

H. Wren

Listen to the Wren's song

And your heart

Will overflow.

Indigo

Sweet violet

Your purple

Touches me

Deeply

Portals

Open the Door

Open the Gate

Lay down your burdens

Lay down your hate

Take up the Staff

Take up the Power

Walk into the Garden

Each moment

Each hour

Sunrise

A new day

Has been born

Within me

And everything

Is fresh

And green

And sparkling

With drops of dew

Foundation

Build slow

Build stead

Build in rhythm

With the moonbeams

Upon the ocean night

The Hum of Growth

Is heard in the void

Between the stars

Listen and Build

Build steady

Build slow

Surfeit

As I read the Holy Scripture

With deeper levels of my Being

Each word becomes

A book unto itself

Balance

Set the course

And journey

Straight ahead

Into the core

Neither left

Nor right

But Center

All the Way

Centrifugal Force

Go out and

It flees from you

Be still and

It comes to Center

The Great Adventure

I do not want

To travel anywhere

But into the Vast Regions

Of the Heart

Of my Beloved

Companionship

At the beginning of the day

I looked alone across the bay

At the day's end

I looked once more

But with a friend

Flow

All I have to be is me

All I have to do is Be

And that's true creativity

Vision

The Single Eye

Sees clearly

The double eye

As through a glass darkly

One

It excites me so

To know that

I am One with all

And that the spark in me

Is the same as that

Which makes

The forget-me-not

So unforgettable

Fear

What I fear the most

Would be my greatest liberator

If I could only yield to it

And allow it to crack the shell

Of my lower self

Curriculum

If I wanted to learn to fly

I'd ask a bird to teach me

For swimming, a fish

I would employ

But to learn the Secrets of Soul

To a garden

A Garden in Kumur

I would go

Research Scientist

I want to go deep within

The laboratory of my Being

And discover

The Secret of Life

Till Harvest Time

In my garden I will plant

Flowers of Spirit

And water them with Life

I will provide them

With Light and Love

And when they are ready

I will give them away

The Way

My soul sings

Of bygone days

And centuries in Eternity

Where it gathered and garnered the Lessons

Which brought it to

The Is-ness of Now

Years seem as mere drops of water

Compared with Lifetimes of Soul

And Eternity becomes

The ever-present Way

All I want to do

Is to Be

The Way

In the Way

Of the Eternal

The Way of Dharma

Life is a River

Ever flowing, ongoing

Slowly, steadily

From Eternity to Eternity

All persons bathe in its waters

At all times

Let the current carry you

Offer no resistance

For only then

Can you pass into and out of

Your lessons with ease

Collector

Joy is so precious

It bubbles forth

And breaks upon the noonday

As ocean waves

Upon a sandy shore

Collecting sea shells

Is a poor substitute

For gathering

The Joy of the Heavens

The Gardener

I have a garden

In my consciousness

And in it I want to plant

Seeds which will grow

Into a glorious bounty

For my Lord

Weeding is an activity

That I must work at

Wholeheartedly

Divisions

Between the world and me

Is an envelope of flesh

Between God and me

Is a state of Consciousness

Formula

Ignorance – not knowing

Knowledge – knowing

Wisdom – knowing and doing

Mandala

A rose is a Mandela

In every sense

Pharmacopoeia

Knowledge is a stimulant

Love, a relaxant

Wisdom, a balance of the above

Travel

Why should I sail the sea

When I can fly in my heart

Basic Ecology

Clean your head up

And you clean the world up

Not vice versa

Visitor

When I see you coming

I hear

Wind chimes

Royal Purple

The new dimension

Deserves mention

It is gentian

That gets our attention

In the new dimension

Altitude

Higher than a kite

Soars the I of my heart

War

The Killer

And the Killed

Are One –

How pointless!

Interconnectedness

We manifested forms

Are focal points

In the Vast Network

Of the Universe

Inebriation

My heart is wine country

The vineyards are God's

Universal I

My eye is a globe

Planet Earth is an eye

And God is the

Third eye

Beyond Thought

With my mind intact

And my heart in tow

I go, I go, I go

With my heart intact

And my mind in tow

I fly, I fly, I fly

Eternal Now

I must be living

In a kaleidoscope

For every moment

I turn around

Everything changes

New color

New wonder

New joy

New delight

Simplicity

To be free

I must

Be

Me

Autumn
Season of Transmutation

Whoever thought

That green turns gold

Within the Mother load

Of my Heart

Hope

Life can begin anew

At any moment

We reach up and accept

The Waters from Heaven

Springtime

There is time

Among the apple boughs

The burgeoning of Spring

For new beginnings

Dormant seeds and those misplaced

Can renew themselves and multiply

Seeking nature's greening

And the fertile pastures

Of the Far Country

Springtime

Nothing is ever lost –

Only transmuted

Nature's harmonies are ever present

And the Song sings through all

And weaves together Life's Symphony

Bend as the rushes in the wind

Flow with the Stream of Life

Reach up and accept

The Waters of Heaven

The Song of Songs

Springtime

Let it flow through you

And break the sod for crocuses

Be Spring

There is time

Open

Deep in my heart

There is a world apart

From any I have ever known

Come walk with me in my garden

Promise not to change

Anything you see

And I will show you all

That means everything to me

Talents

If I had but one string

On my violin

I would learn how to play

A symphony upon it

For my Lord

Change

I have changed

And all I want to do

Is to sing Hymns of Silver

And Psalms of Gold

And offer frankincense and myrrh

And Praise forever more

To my Lord

The Giver of All Gifts

Change

He is like the rising Sun

And warms my whole Being

With Light and Love

And gently encourages it

To grow upward to meet Him

He is green and lush

Like a new born plant

And gives me succor

Which I could never hope to find

In ten thousand midnights without Him

Change

He is merciful and kind

And yet quick and firm

In His Discipline

He is a Way Shower

And a Teacher of teachers

I would like to sing

Songs of Praise to Him

For Eternity

For He is my very Life

And all that I do is from Him

He is the author of my New Self

Change

He has filled me to overflowing

With new vintage

It is sweet and pure

And is not of this Earth

Come sup with me

For I want to share these

Many blessings with you

I have a bounty of Joy in me

That could flow into

Eternity Forever

Change

Comes up with me

And I will give you Joy

For It was given me to share

And share I must

For it is too much for me alone to bear

It is too sweet, too lovely, too pure

To keep in one's embrace

Let us sup together

In the Joy of the Lord

And Sing Him praise

Forevermore

Pastoral

He saw her by the stream

And gently laid His Hand upon her head

She was intent in watching

The fishes swim upon

The colored stones

Between the moss

And jump at insects

Here and there

She watched the circles ever expand

And felt complete Oneness with Nature

And the Joy of Being

Spiritual Vanity

I have bathed in the Waters

And in my Soul

I know the Secrets of Eternity

I have been richly blessed

And am awaiting my Work

In hopes that I may still

Be found worthy

In spite of my trespasses against Spirit

And the blackness I conjured up

In my vast ignorance

I feel as old as Time itself

And find my circumstance

Spiritual Vanity

Here upon the Earth Plane

Strange and foreign to my Being

I never fit here

Because my roots were in Heaven, you see,

And I never quite seemed to

Make the transplant in its entirety

But tell me now

I have my lessons to learn

To wake the Soul to Its full height

I, too, like everyone else

Must learn the lessons

Step by step

Spiritual Vanity

And make mistakes

And fall and arise

To fall again and rise again

To someday walk

Steadily upon the Path

Without resistance

Our Land

I am America

I sing my Song

To the Nations of the World

I am the melting pot of humanity

And the Light of the Earth

I have born within my boundary lines

The Teachers of the Coming Age

They will show a New Way

And the people will rejoice and change

And build up Life anew

And our Planet will become

A blessing unto the Universe

Multi-Racial Baby

I am the Child of the Golden Race

In my blood flows the history of all nations

I am the world itself

My ancestors were the benefactors

Of the race of man

I am the brother of all and to all

For your father is my father

And your mother, my mother

I speak the language of all men

And am at home in all countries

I have worshipped at every altar

And have been welcomed into every faith

Multi-Racial Baby

But my body is my temple

And the Lord is my Shepherd

At the Core of Everywoman

I am the Mona Lisa

Within my heart is the Secret of Secrets

I have peace within me

To give succor to the whole of mankind

The milk from my breast flows freely

I have joy within me

To sing His Song forever

My smile is but His Love upon my lips

My eyes have seen the Glories of Glories

And the Light of Lights

My ears have heard the Music of the Spheres

I am one with All

At the Core of Everywoman

The Mother of the Universe

Come unto me and I will give thee

Love and Light

And Peace and Joy

For Eternity

Above Duality

I am the mountain in the snow

And the snowflake in the air

I am the eagle and the dove

I am the butterfly and the cocoon

I am the end and the Beginning

I am all things to everyone

I am the Evil and the Good

I am laughter and tears

I am death and life

I am the hunter and the hunted

I am the weak and the strong

I am the wise and the fool

Above Duality

I am the brave and the fearful

I am the rich and the poor

I am the saint and the sinner

I am the child and the man

I am the tyrant and the slave

I am the cultured and the ignorant

I am the humble and the brash

I am the bright and the dull

I am all men of all nations

And of all faiths and all beliefs

I am the feast and famine

I am the acorn and the oak

Above Duality

I am the forest and the desert

I am the sun and the moon

I am the zephyr and the hurricane

I am the dewdrop and the ocean

I am all things seen and unseen

I am the fingers and the hand

I am the unicorn and the ape

I am the Light and the Dark

I am Forever for Eternity

I am indestructible

For I am All in All

Awake

Above Duality

And Know

I AM

Song

In your face I see

The mystery of all there was

And evermore will be

Your eyes are like the sea

So filled with life

And deep enough for me

To feel all your love

Song

You're real

And somehow

When I'm with you

I'm living wholly in the NOW

There are too few of us

Who reach the point within

Where we can see

What is Divine

And taste the fruit

Fresh from the Living Vine

Song

My love

I feel so safe with you

I pray that you will never part

From the garden

Hidden deep within my heart

In this secret place

I always see your face

Shining down upon me

Warm as sun upon the sea

Song

Your eyes embrace me with your love

And fill me like

The symbol of the dove

With Peace

Antique Lady

There was an old antique lady

Who lived down by the sea

Where she counted empty jam jars

And her tarnished jewelry

She'd sit by the window

Sipping blueberry tea

As she savored and flavored

Each fond memory

Antique Lady

She loved to go rocking

In her rocking chair

And count all the gulls

In the warm salty air

She'd laugh and she'd whisper

To people unseen

Who peopled her house

And her thinking machine

Antique Lady

She spent her days gently

Like old-fashioned silk

And wove her nights warmly

With brandy and milk

She was a beautiful soul

Serene as could be

Living her life

By the edge of the sea

Beware

I am Chief Standing Bear

Chief of the Wapello

Beware

The Earth is in danger

Even the dove cries out

Return to the great One

Or suffer the fires of Eternity

You have turned our land into a desert

And our ocean into a cesspool

Beware

The Earth Mother is slow to anger

But she is awakening

Beware

And rumbling deep within

Change your ways

O Mighty Nation

Or She will split your gut with terror

For her wrath is great

Beware

Seven Moons of Uranus

(In memoriam to voyagers of the

Challenger Space Shuttle—January 28, 1986)

Heroes and Heroines

Icarian Space Gods of 20th Century America

Broken Wings without Feathers

We salute you for your Spirit of Adventure

For your Courage

For your Pursuit of Excellence

For uniting our hearts

We embrace you skyward

Valiant Ones

Seven Moons of Uranus

We fly with you

Through Eternity

Red Man Speaks

I am Chief Yellow Hawk

I have returned with my son, Running Deer

And his mother Susquehanna

We have come again

To claim our land

And raise the dead

We have for too long

Been in mourning

Witnessing the destruction

Of our Earth Mother

We have come to give freedom

To all those who hear our call

Red Man Speaks

We come as peacemakers, not as warlords

We have come to bring New Life into this land

All the forests of our country

Will be for people to enjoy

The lakes will be for all to bathe in

We will teach man to live

In harmony with the land

The people will again cherish the soil

And treat it with respect

The animals will come out of hiding

And will roam freely

The Passenger Pigeon shall rise up

Red Man Speaks

And fly again

Over the land without harm

And the buffalo will graze the Prairie

The wheat and corn

Will grow from nature's own

The skies will clear and people

Will return to handicrafts

All will worship the Great Father

And the Earth Mother

The children will laugh and smile again

The lion will lay down with the lamb

And peace will reign in our Land

Meltdown

Fatal cloud of Chernobyl

Loosed upon

An unsuspecting world

Altering genetic codes and changing destiny

For untold generations

Yet to be born

Affecting members of Plant and

Animal Kingdoms alike

Stop

Think

Re-evaluate

Halt the madness

Meltdown

Admit defeat

Seek alternatives

There is no time for delusion, ego, greed

Citizens of the Earth are waiting

Stop

Deception

Montessori, they call her

I call her Freedom

High priestess

Of the Essence

To teach is to touch the soul

To induce it to dance with you

And to allow it to expand into

All dimensions

Deception

Oh, How many souls

Are galvanized for life

By those who call themselves

''Teacher.''

Yes

Sweep my room clean, Lord

Purify the water

Let the breeze flow clear through

And the note sound pure

Sweep my room, Lord

I am ready to share my abode

Nay, not share

But gift it empty

In Thy Service

Yes

Show me the Way to go Home, Lord

Take me through the Eye of the Needle

Yes

To the Inner Chambers and the many mansions

Teach me, discipline me wholly

In Your time, Lord, in Your time

Yes, I am a borning and a becoming

Yes

Yes, Lord, I say yes

Yes to pain, yes to joy

Yes to poverty, yes to riches

Yes to thirst, yes to slake

I say yes, Lord

And with every yes, I say yes, Lord

Yes, yes, yes

Yes

And then yes

And with each and every yes, Lord

Thank You

Hearts are open places and open spaces

Temple rooms of worship and praise

Hearts are full of poetry and music

Hearts are overflowing

With yeses and thanksgiving

Yes

All this behind doors of unknowingness

Melt my heart, Lord

Hold the key as I unlock the door

Yes

The treasure is Yours

Yes, yes, yes

And thank You

Yes

Sanctuary of Beingness

High in the mountains

Spectacular to view

Ecstatic beauty

Is waiting for you

Bubbling Spring

With sacred Sound

Sourcing the Symphony

Heard all around

Sanctuary of Beingness

My cup runneth over

And spills into the stream

I am awake

But it seems like a dream

Let me dance in the meadow

Alive with song

Among brooks and flowers

This is where I belong

Sanctuary of Beingness

High in the mountains

Kissing the sky

Drinking pure water

How blessed am I

Varied species of birds

Flit to and fro

With a freedom and grace

We would love to know

Sanctuary of Beingness

Dance in the Energy

Dance in the Sound

Dance with the Nature Spirits

That everywhere abound

Visit the Meadow

In dream or for real

Come along, come along

Dance, sing, and heal

Sanctuary of Beingness

I am wealthy beyond measure

Having come upon this site

And assimilated its essence

Its majesty and might

In gratitude I leave it

But only physically

For it will nourish me forever

Mind, soul, emotion -- all three

Final Words

"What lies behind us and what lies before us are tiny matters compared to what lies within us."

—Ralph Waldo Emerson

About the Author

After working many years in the public sector Nadja is reinventing herself as an artist and writer. She has an eclectic background. Her joys include adventuring on the Open Road, dancing, cooking, being in nature, writing and painting. She is also interested in natural building, organic gardening, alternative health, life-long learning, travel, and living moment to moment. Nadja writes for the conscious community and people who are interested in healing, meditation, transformation, ascension, and the New Earth. This includes highly sensitive people, Starseeds, Indigos, empaths, Light Workers, energy healers, artists, visionaries, and those in recovery and discovery.

Also by Nadja

Soft-cover books, eBooks, MP3s, and CDs, Smashwords, Amazon, Kindle, CreateSpace, CDBaby, iTunes, YouTube, and your local bookstore by request.

River of Living Light

Evolution Revolution

Random Thoughts and Poems

Hopi Blue Corn

El Maiz Azul de los Hopis

Visionary Tales for the New Earth

Color Me Bright Coloring Book

Blue Sky

Ascension Codes

Raps, Chants, and Rants

Women's Power Awakened

Ozzengoggle Poems

From the City of Shem

You Are Not Alone

Family Secrets

Flying Heart

Bullies

www.ingramcontent.com/pod-product-compliance
Lightning Source LLC
Chambersburg PA
CBHW070811050426
42452CB00011B/1998